Everything Awake

Sasha Steensen

EVERYTHING AWAKE

Shearsman Books

First published in the United Kingdom in 2020 by
Shearsman Books Ltd
PO Box 4239
Swindon
SN3 9FN

Shearsman Books Ltd Registered Office
30–31 St. James Place, Mangotsfield, Bristol BS16 9JB
(this address not for correspondence)

www.shearsman.com

ISBN 978-1-84861-710-0

CONTENTS

Come, you hendecasyllables, in force now,
each last one of you, from every quarter—

—Catullus

Hende

The opposite of wakefulness is not sleep.
Neither the day nor the night can be said to speak
without me. I open my mouth and out shines
the horizon. It hums no matter the time.
It forms the seam between dawn and dreams. No matter
the lilies or the nightshade. All we say to sleep—
please, allusive friend, freeze. All our offerings—
the sawed log, the leaped fence, the sheep. None of it matters.
Like Telemachos wrapped in fleece, sweet sleep doesn't
hold me. Obedient, I wait for radiant dawn.
I hold myself still. I lay myself down.

Practicing in the Sleepfields

Well past twilight now.

Go your ways in the black ship,
I tell myself as I lay myself down.

Then, I take a walk.

The raccoon
circling the coop
barely looks at me.

The baby skunk
hunting grubs
in the garden
doesn't lift his tail up.

My cat
with a mouse
in her mouth.

New moon
in the distance.

Polaris.

Orion.
His armpit.
His belt doesn't fit.

I'm tired
of myself.

I lie myself down
on the dewy ground.

*

I prefer the word
weary
how it drives
what rides me
(worry)
out past the waves
most noteworthy
and leaves me bedridden
on a glassy sea.

This is what it feels like,
the verge of sleep,
lulling up and down
gently
on what we call
the wave's trough.

There is no feed for me.
No oats.
No grain.
No hay.

Seed,
out to sea.

*

Twilight means
the great between,

but there is more to day
than dark and light

more to twi-
than half or twice.

Blue horizon,
what shall we call thee?
Intrinsic light isn't quite right,
nor is Eigengrau

Eigenlicht
own gray
dark light.

Paul tells us to fear the dark,
to wear the armor of light.

What's that, bright
in the dark distance?

The night's nightcap,
I guess.

I put it atop my windy head
and rest.

*

I write this in the early morning
ambien ambient daze
and what's worse,
that gray brain

or having not slept
in the first place?

I ask myself this until the end
of what we call day.
Nightfall, eventide, decline,
in India, cow dust time.

Thou dost sweep men away like a dream.
And the dust from their hooves
and the smoke from our nightfire rises.

I'm too unsure of my place
in the waking day
to find my way
back home with my cows in tow.

In the dream,
the image does its work effortlessly,
but upon waking,
there is no shore to be seen.

What keeps me most afloat:
the echoes of words.

*

Sitting down to work,
I almost immediately
require a nap.

For seven mornings straight
this nap occurs from 10:52 to 11:08.

This is what the Hebrews called
"the casual sleep."

The time it takes
to walk ¾ of a mile
elongated and stretched out
above the quiet house.

This morning
I heard a fly buzz
when I fell asleep
and again when I woke.

The nap:
one continuous moment.

*

Seven sleepers sleep in a cave in Ephesus
for one-hundred-nine-thousand-five-hundred-some days.
Or 309 lunar years, give or take.
The sleepers believe they've only slept
a portion of one day.

The "seventh sleeper" means:
sleeping late, being lazy,
or having faith.

The seventh sleeper
also refers
to the edible dormouse
(from the word dormīre)
who hibernates for seven
months a year.

The rodent has seven teats in Italy
but only six elsewhere.

If we were ancient Romans,
we'd trap and fatten
these rodents
in terracotta pots
until plump enough for roasting.

If we were German,
we'd celebrate
not Ground Hog's Day,
but Seven Sleeper's Day.
If wet, it will rain
for seven weeks
without rest.

If we were Syrian, we'd bless
one another with the following words:
May you sleep like the people of Ephesus.

The weather and little rodents both
speak to me.

Dawn over the sea.
The boat's hull.
The husk of sleep.

If my arms could reach down
and pull you out,
if my mouth could breathe
for thee.

*

Like the jaw aching to open wide
at the sight of a yawning child,
eyes reading about sleep
grow heavy.

I bow my head to the book.

Reading.

For the insomniac,
reading is the gentle guillotine.

I want the honey-hearted sleep,
the sleep that takes the shape
of a swarm of bees
humming
longsuffering,
lovingkindness,
safekeeping,
alone in my bed
of blue poppies always in bloom,
God breathing the dream into me.

Reading.

Sleep that fans like a whirlwind
cools like a mist
set me off to sea
by way of the winds released
from goat skins.
Sleep that isn't sleep exactly
but brings me to the bed
nonetheless.
And sleep in which the sleeper dreams
she is sleeping

but can't, whatever she does,
wake herself up.

Reading.

Blocking a hole.
Stopping a breach.
Patching a garment.
The boat on a rough sea,
the olive tree,
the bed upon which Penelope sleeps.

Reading.

I know I slept.
I have a pain
in my neck,
a dry eye
that aches
to open
and an
unfinished book
by my bed.

Late May.

My fifteenth wedding anniversary.

There are children between him and me
and we roll out the bed and ready them.

*

Until my girl was a year old,
she barely slept. She
only slept
in someone's arms or
in her babyswing.

When she finally learned to sleep
in her crib, I would wake
on my floormat where I slept
when I couldn't sleep
wondering why
she wasn't crying.

I would worry that perhaps
she had died in her sleep,
but then I would tell myself,
go back to sleep
because if she's dead,
grief will prevent you
from ever sleeping again.

*

The vigil in hypervigilant:

rising to someone who sleeps
like a dream or seems asleep
even upon waking, the misty
eyes, the talk that is itself
the words of one asleep
who assumes I know the scene
of whatever dream he's still
half dreaming.

And rising to someone
who, two hours asleep,
reaches a delta,
opens her eyes and screams.
Knowing its better to be witness
to night terrors, and not speak,
I look into her open eyes
but she doesn't see me.
I whisper, *please,* quietly,
and immediately
she becomes a broody hen
who won't let me in
to fetch the egg
and calm the wind.

And rising to someone
whose mouth is too small
to get the air she needs,
someone whose tonsillectomy
made space where none existed
but still,
her weighty breath finds me,
like a leaf vein, its stem,
restless in my own bed.

And rising to other creatures
who sleep standing up
who sleep on a giant spool
under the full moon
who sleep roosting in the rafters
who sleep under an infrared light
until they feather out
who sleep on a log
under an artificial sun
scheduled to go on

each morning
at 6:43
who hunt mice instead of sleep
who ravage my flock instead of sleep
who chirp in their cricket keeper
until they become the lizard's dinner.

I cannot sleep
unless / because
I hear my offspring.

Meanwhile, we have four nests
around the house,
some with babies,
some with eggs,
some without:

2 Magpie
1 Robin
1 Finch with a cuckoo egg
upon which the mamabird
sleeps unknowingly

until she flies away
leaving all the eggs

nestled
together.

*

When I can't sleep
I long to live

somewhere other
than here

where
even the weeds
make noise
as they sleep.

Somewhere
where people
wander
at night
aimlessly,
like me.

When I can't sleep
and I have an idea
I get up and go to my computer
which needs awakened
from its deep sleep.
I frantically whip
the mouse around.
I bring my entire palm down
on the keys.

Eventually, the computer
wakes reluctantly
and accepts my idea.

When I can't sleep,
I recite the prayer
Now I lay me down to sleep
I pray the Lord my soul to keep
And if I die before I wake

I pray the Lord my soul to
                              make. remake.
                              mistake
                              me

for someone already held gently
in the tender arms of sleep and leave.

*

The urn
in nocturnal
is also
a turn.

By which I mean,
sleep is one-sixteenth part death.

It's death's doorknob, locked
from the inside out.

I am on my knees
poking at the hole
with the tiniest of
screwdrivers
until the click
wakes me.

Our belief that we can be happy
is first formed during sleep.
When we wake and find
that we've merely been dreaming
we fall to our knees in misery.

Sleep, in which we practice many things, among them:
birthing, forgetting, writing, leaving, sewing,
working, waking, but most of all, dying.

Gloaming is a noun
that sounds like a verb.
Sleep is a thing we learn
by doing.

Which means, when death comes to me,
I will be exceedingly bad at it.

*

The gods wanted to stay in bed forever
so they gave us each
a mass of souls,
only one of which sleeps.
The rest do the gods' work
all the day and all the night long.

Like Telemachus,
wrapped in a sheep fleece,
I do the work of worry.

The sea and sleep
are far from me
and the prairie near.
I may be deep in error
and as brief as an atom,
but worry and hope both
belong to expectancy.

Sleep's root,
deep like a weed,
is not in this world.

In the dark night
I bend down
and feel around
for the thistle spreading
chocking out
all else.

I pull
as close
to the ground
as I can.

I rend.

Sheepfold.
Cocklight.

I call my creatures
in for the night.

Hendes First

1.

Last night I found a robin in the garage.
This morning, she is still there, and a finch
has joined her. They shit everywhere. The children
are giddy and also not listening. Not
putting their boots on not zipping their coats not
moving their bikes not getting along not
climbing into that shitty car, certainly not
until I clean it off. They flap their wings. Not
not crying, they look at me. The radio says, today
this rain will turn to snow. Today, mid-
September in Northern Colorado.

2.

The o shone. The sun, I mean. The o sang
itself whole before the horizon, so loud
we could not see, but louder still the he-
goat in rut whu whu whuing and smelling of
himself so strongly. This dawn we have it in air
even acres away. Muskrat in creek, she-
goat in heat. We in the mountain's armpit see
east o lift the valley's mist. He drinks his own
piss and bathes in it. Presumably she'll find him
becoming. Fierce it is and sharp of note.
O oestrus bit: the goat and the goatherd both.

3.

Into the place of production, I bring seams,
words, foods, bodies, even the hands I made
make things and it feels we might wait, we might
rest easy here for this while. All else goes
on outside and we nearly miss it. Scarcely
below the roots of some vegetables, it lies.
By the river, the corpse of an hour, it asks us:
what happened here. It's nothing more than a single moment,
and a large part of the earth is still
an urn to us. You know how the imagination
makes its way to death instantaneously, almost.

4.

When I write the word *walnut,* fear, curled,
like the crevices of that nut's vulva, unfurls.
If I see one at the grocery store, I freeze,
I look for my little girl, I listen to her breathe.
I want to wrap its green husk, Wealhhnutu,
"foreign nut," back around it and let it rest,
forever. When she wants to know how loved
she is, she sings a song of questions, "would you,
my mother, ever let a walnut in this house?"
"No, never," I tell her. "Would you, my mother, ever
let its tree grow by my porch?" "No, never," I tell her.

5. (sleep restriction therapy)

I lie awake. I am like a lonely bird
on a rooftop about to leap off. This is not
a simile. I'm exhausted from delousing the house.
A sparrow can't fall to the ground apart from God.
She is worth more than an entire flock.
And even the very nits on her head are counted:
two-hundred-eleven. I watch the hatched bugs crawl off.
At school, she's just finished a unit on habitats:
hair, skin, debris and blood. She's thrilled to use a word
she's just learned: *parasite.* The way we live
and thrive. My ear an entrance she can reach,
an entrance into which she screams her needs,
and miraculously, the host delivers
water, food, a movie. The host combs and preens.
The host wraps up dying bugs for two weeks.
The host vacuums and alerts friends we've seen recently.
The host hides under the table and weeps.
The host puts her own head to rest finally,
and if she sleeps, she dreams of a thousand heads
in the house, bodiless, laying themselves down
on pillows, beds, rugs, all teeming with bugs
and scavenging thoughts that keep her from sleep.

6.

Because I want the day to say something to me,
squeak-squeak, I mistake the neighbor's bike horn
for a rare bird. I've begun dreaming again
and now I run from them. I must be weary
of finding the goats' heads severed by the stream.
I must be like a daylily, the tree's shadow,
the frost in the shape of an evergreen. The sun
ever coming coming gone. I must do laundry.
I am in ecstasy. Truly, the windfucker
is a bird. It beat its wings heartily home.
Six loads interfere with the poem.

7. (sleep restriction therapy)

All else I leave weedy because of futility.
How we send "light" when our friends are in pain
or mourning. How we wish for more hours
in a day. I want the day to recede
and I want darkness, but no one sends these.
I waste time because I have it to throw away.
I dust. I take surveys. I try to decide
if my snoring child needs a tonsillectomy.
I post a status update, then I press delete.
I pick a fight and beg you not to leave me. By me,
I mean the poem; it is our home.
I curse myself and open the windows.
I turn the radio on low and the lights on
high. I plead and I cry. I read the same lines
repeatedly: Whoever has read *The Prairie*
Flower Or, Adventures in the Far West will see
that it's spoken of as a spot of eventful meaning
but instead of "eventful," I read eventually,
and then, almost inexplicably, "very poor
grasses." If you stay with me, I've a garden,
and a goat and a chicken. We will eat.
All else I leave weedy because of futility.

8.

Into a field of old Walsingham, I wish
my bones might lie soft, the earth be light upon them.
Snow resting vertical on the laundry line
does not let go, holds what we need most: socks without holes.
The child will not go to school with these socks,
no she will not! I take my crooked pin
out my mouth and darn them. Either some evil
eye bewitched my tender lambs or I sheared them close
too late in the season, they freeze, their cloven
hooves bleed. At the threshold, daddy screams:
tardy things! and all-teary, they leave.

9.

It seems we cannot step beyond the everyday.
The line moves slowly but persistently, it sways
in the traffic's breeze, blown toward me and then
away. The child tells me she wants to go quietly,
minding her own business. Out walking she may
wait to cross the street until the everyday
is swept up from the curb. We work to earn our leisure
and leisure has only one meaning—to get away
from work. That leisure is a critique
of the everyday makes pleasure a snake
coiling itself closer by coiling away.

10. (sleep restriction therapy)

It having dropped twenty degrees, the chicks are
in my office with me. I watch them watch
each other sleep. The word they speak is their eyes
growing heavy. It means, I am with thee.
It means they are as one body speaking,
with their beaks, of the bounty of sleep. It seems everywhere
beckoning me, but I cannot
go through to the other side. I would do
so much to be in its grips, to hold firmly
the syllables one meets while asleep.
I cannot keep them open in its midst but
I must. I even type this with them shut.
Hypnos shook my hand once and now my beloved
is a nap I cannot take. I must be kept
awake and already the bed's shape
lightens, its shadow lengthens, not just
as the day proceeds because that would be
too easy. Noonday and midnight equally
want me, but I plant my feet firmly
on the ground of waking. That which I had
come to hate keeps me company until the body
echoes back the stillness it sees in the last chick's peep.

11.

Something like day unto day utters speech
Or night unto night reveals knowledge, or
snow so light today, it floats up each and every
way. Ice is to tire as slippery is
to anxiety. Just below freezing, a sheet
of water between. My daughter on a bus,
weaving in and out, headed down the mountain.
She's fine, but what about the neighbor's neighbor, found
dead on the ground. Each tragedy says foolishly:
be not anxious for the morrow, for the morrow
will be anxious for the things of itself.

12.

Taking oneself to be less and less important
by engaging oneself all the more, like a toddler
tantruming on the floor. The day forgave
the burden of self-care, undoubtedly
the most difficult to bear. I imagine
myself a whale whose brain only half sleeps
so that she might continue to breathe. I'm not one
to be in the night easily nor to give ear
to the silent e in bee. I'm not one even.
I'm plenty and too many, the infection
echoing *be*. Its humming relieves my sleep.

13.

Some days I can't believe you are my child,
How tremendously beautiful your eye, the one
that now, unpatched, works, and your itchy skin is.
At your preschool, they don't call letters
by their names, but their sounds, my favorite being
w-uh. W-uh means so many things, doesn't it? W-uh
means the beginning of questioning and
the answer too. When I prepare a meal
in an eggshell, I wait for you ask, what's
in there? Where? We set the table. I worry
you'll be left out, making sounds no one understands.
And now your small mouth needs expanded. Please,
don't vanish into it.

14.

The neighbor boy screams a scream I can't ignore
and yet I do because he is not mine.
And now he's ringing my doorbell incessantly
and I ignore that too. He wants my daughters,
but they aren't home and I can't answer for them.
 And now he's at the backdoor knocking, and now
he's readying his convertible kid car. Soon,
he'll be in my garage. I'm weary.
Walking up the steps, I think, these are my feet
walking up the steps. No, this is me, walking
my feet up the steps. To think of myself can be
so very boring. I try to stop for a while.
And I succeed! I'm asleep!

15.

If you crush the bergamot heads with your feet
you find your way forward not by seeing.
If you clean the coop with the new broom
you find no room for the mulched leaves.
If you compost everything but meat
you can't find the accidentally discarded thing.
If you have come undone in order to be reached
you find weeds endlessly becoming. If you
hunt and skin the deer, if you sew the pelt,
you find relief, as when the needle, felt
instead of seen, makes its way up from the underseam.

16. (sleep restriction therapy)

Thoughts last night like the geese we see, each taking
their turn at the upwash. Hundreds of them.
I don't know what a formation is, the skein
so untangled in the air, a layering
of v's. My girl and I watch until we can't
see the last straggler, until we can't hear
the honking. They know a place warmer, water
frozen only at the banks. They want the sideways
light. They want the day longer than the night,
and softer. That's why they fly just barely above
the goose in front. *How they must love each other,*
how they work together! my girl says, impressed
with what she calls their *thoughtfulness.* We tip our heads
toward the ground again to collect the goat dung
for the garden. Hundreds of them.
In Chinese poetry, a single goose means
one of two things: if wild, exile;
if domesticated, marriage. One worry
falls back and another takes the lead until
I'm asleep. In the dream, a gaggle of geese
on the ground feeding, is one thought finally,
and it means rest, it means continue breathing.

17.

Today is one hour less than the day before.
The Northern Flicker returns, pecking its beak
at a rapid pace on any metal place. How many
dogs' barks remain unheard? How many
birds' chirps? How many tests we complete
in each waking and each going to sleep.
The lost hour unfurls predictably, not
unlike the diurnal movements of the tamarind tree.
Or rather, of its leaves. Perhaps its little
seeds prefer the moist soil of day. I might
too, would noon be doubled, a pod split in two.

18.

She's nine years old today and *half-way-to*
-out-of-here I hear her say. I hold tight
 the hyphen as if it is a lifeboat.
She gives me two duck feathers plucked from their blue
necks. White-tipped downy and purple in the house
-light. She's in love with their guts, which one ate sand
and which one ate none, because they will taste of it.
Long gathered the animals we bring to our lips.
He's field dressing them in the snow, and every
cell sits still. Not hers alone. I go uphill
with two duck feathers in my shame-pocket tucked.

19.

I wonder if this breeze might really be
a boat, a little rowboat with a little bench,
a little bench with a little notch straight from
the little tree that grew in the little grove,
the little grove outside the wintery city,
the wintery city from which the breeze
must have blown. The middle of this poem,
for some many months, remained empty.
But the sunlight hasn't just been sitting
there quietly. It's been blowing also.
Life *is* fair, the breeze that brings the snow.

20.

Pronghorn pronghorn pronghorn pronghorn pronghorn prong
horn. We don't have gazelles here but antelope nor wolves
but foxes nor do we have eyes to see well
because we've got a tear in one, not the kind
that waters but a rip made by my little babe.
I like the word from whence it came: Fray.
I've got a fray in my eye and each night,
if I sleep straight through the lid becomes so intimate
with this little rip that to break those ties
is to rewound the eye. Just keep it shut
all the time else the day feels like the pronghorn's name.

21. (sleep restriction therapy)

Too soon, the earth moved. Too soon, the acorn
of light, its little hat tipped. Too soon, Nyx
laid her brilliant white egg on the boundless lap.
Too soon it hatched. Too soon Phanes's golden wing
a prism. Too soon the rooster out the coop,
his black beak a V blowing the moon west,
 too soon his kukuku, too soon, his cock-a-
snake wrapped around the egg the hen laid too soon.
Too soon the mountains red. Too soon the dream
in which we swim ends. Too soon my body—
feet spread and strapped, back-passage widely gaped—closes.
Too soon you recede, walking backwards.
Too soon, the ache at each opening. Too soon
the morn. Too soon my eyelash catches sight of it—
a net, a spider web, a briar patch. Too soon
the dew gone. Too soon, the thirst of every pore.
Too soon, little feet. Too soon, little hands.
Too soon, little palms shaking me awake.
Too soon, little whispers in my ear.
Too soon, my eye sees the umber of its lid.
Too soon, it sees its opposite.
Too soon, the wind-sown egg from whence we came.

22.

This is the insomnia note I didn't
leave last night. It is the night I didn't
sleep through. It is the day that wrote itself
asleep and bloomed whole-heartedly. The heart
I wake to. I am, as far as I am able,
a phantom. I set my foot in God's mouth.
I climb in and we swim. We waters wash
over you, you who sleep soundly all above.
I call an assembly of yous so that I
might not be alone in this darkness
this which is oh so welcome and beyond.

Noonday Prayers

The day always
opens wide,

always
peers inside.

Always wants
to know

what is near,
far & wide

& also
what makes
the crops rejoice,
beneath what star to plough,
and when to wed the vines to elms.

I ask the hands I hold
I ask the emerald
I ask the breath and the depth.

You can ask the rooster and the hen.
Though their wings span the breadth,
you can capture them.
You can hold them in your hands.
You can press them to your breast.

I have done as much and they haven't struggled.
So too the lamb, the goat, the fatted calf.

Ask them.

But can the soul,
once gone,
be captured back?

Ask the dry stalks.
Ask the rattling pods.

*

I sleep and wake
to another way

in mind. There are friends
I ask. And children.

There are tasks I ask.
And plants.

I ask
the winter rye

it says I

      feed upon
      what will come come spring

      and it isn't only you
      who sing.

      The rooster too.

I ask the morrow.
It says, no,

> I won't
> take care
> of myself

and yet
I am not without
hope.

*

My girl holds one egg
up to her eye to ask

if its been fertilized.

Light shines through
glair and yolk both.

In this way, no egg
is singular once separated.

It being Sunday,
I thank the oysters

who gave their shells
to the chickens

who gave their eggs
to me.

I ask
the word

compensate.

I feel its weight
in either hand.

It says,

>   For some, I come all by myself
>   For others, with a friend.

*

I ask the plot of spreading sunchokes
none can eat

and in my cheek
a loanword stuck.

I ask the little mice lodge,
or is it a colony?

Mass of mice babies
founded in a bin
of chicken feed
made a mess of it.

For some, *mess* means abundance.
For others, there are no means.

I ask my large country.
It says, I've failed.

I've not lifted my lamp
by the golden door.

I've not
a teeming shore.

*

Today I ask the shard of glass
I swept from the kitchen floor.

I press it deep into my palm
and hold it there as if it were dear

to me. The palm throbbing
as I say my prayer.

I clean out
the garbage disposal,

the rotten lime rind,
the bottle cap.

The sound it won't make
when it doesn't rattle.

The ways in which
our compost

can't hold
every piece

of food
we can't eat.

The crisis of which
I am not even

a casualty.

*

I ask that which pleases
merely by being seen,
if it can begin to reseed.

I ask my thought undressed.

It says, Needles make good fodder,
        Father, but my soul is a girl.

Mine too, I sing.
I'm a watchwoman of spring.

I bring my hail bin in
lest the hoes of unkind
hefts find me.

*

What work resists anger
all the day long?

I will not let you go,
lest you tell me.

Lest you bless
the reddish-brown bole

into which we are sown,
and the rain also,

and my cat with two
voles

on her pillow,
and the plum

pollinated by the bee
that previously

pollinated
the birch tree.

*

I ask the moon
so as not

to go to ground
too soon.

I ask the rhubarb high
about the rabbit's eye.

Hornbeam, catkins,
Lamb's quarters,

Goosefoot, Fat-hen.
The fecundity.

I ask the eaves.
I ask Eve.

She says,

>   Sun-up.
>   Night-fall.
>
>   It isn't snowing.
>   The wind is blowing.

*

I ask the geneticist
who produced
a complete map
of the chicken genome.

Gallus gallus domesticus.

I ask the grapes which ripen
on a day when we are away.

I ask the skins and seeds
plump in the birds' bellies.

I ask the daylight
how much its worth
to chip away at ice.

it says,

>   measure the shovel and salt
>   and by your own body
>   divide.

*

Every spring
I ask a whole year's hope.

I ask the unwilling earth.

Tired of me
she says,

>   fate decrees
>   everything
>
>   tumbles into a worse
>   state
>
>   here, grain
>   there, grapes
>
>   olio of seeds,
>   ill omen all.
>
>   Tie your worries
>   round you,

she says,

>   like an ephod,
>   apron of God.

*

The land has its own memory:
the valley.

And also the troposphere.

You can ask them if you like.

You can take your kite
out the garage and tie it tight.
You can speak to its sail.

You can send it up into the air.

You can keep you feet
here

on this dry ground
near all that is dear,

and you can ask that
which swoops down.

The nightingale held
in the hawk's mouth
pleading for its life,

may say,

          she who sings,
          prays twice.

Hendes Second

1.

Today, when it starts to snow, I write a poem
and I stop when it stops. It is very off
and on. The gleaming street too warm to hold it
and wet, like me.
                 Then no word, no thing
but blazing until September when the children
spot the forgotten zucchini and haul it
into the house. It's the size of May, June, July
and August combined. It's the size of my
desire, bitter useless now, we set it
on the lawn where it rots. But still hot, it holds
off the frost, like me, coming coming gone.

2.

The human mind hides from itself, and I find
its hiding place in a grotto or a cave
I find its bedroll and its dried meat I find
its retreat, I find its ancient drawings
of the animal it just slain and the bird head
atop the dying human frame I find
its sex is always erect, even unto death
I find mine quivers at the sight of it I find
that between prehistory and classical antiquity
human sexuality went astray I find
my desire to lay down in its still warm bed and weep.

3.

There are no pots in the large, old house I rent.
 I am meant to be here by myself—to *work*—
but this very word—work (*ergon*)—a friend tells me,
is related, etymologically,
to the Greek word for orgy. Oh, solitary.
I don't know who to ask if excessiveness
better follows company or loneliness.
Or, rather, how to make the gesture of metaphor
without the damn thing catching up with the tenor.
No pots!
I make a hardboiled egg in the microwave.

4.

Most of you already knew what I have just learned,
that amateur simply means lover. I can
hardly believe that part of you kept it from me.
Near a little river you let the chickens out,
and like ducks, they float. As a girl, if I felt
some boy's penis, I mean eyes, upon me
I built a little structure I called boatshedboat.
When I say it fast—boatshedboat—I imagine
you like me or at least you like what I mean. Fuck
Archibald Macleish and meaning and being.
I'm not interested, I mean, interesting.

5.

There may not be a bottom to this
curiosity. There may not be ambergris
in the whale's tummy. We see not day
uttering speech or night revealing anything
but worry. His handiwork looks anxiety
in the face. It has more than a thousand eyes
that dart about. It has two mouths that barely
breathe. It has a hundred hearts each of which beats
sporadically. I look over its shoulder and instantly,
I see what was unforeseen between God and me.
The seam of oblivion smells so sweet.

6. (sleep restriction therapy)

I have a guardian too. To nap with him
or stay awake all day are only two options
he holds behind his back, in his closed hands.
I carry a fan around the house to drown
out the fierce wind, but just now I've
turned it off to write how it sounds: hollow, edge
upon which my body does not rest, fallow sow,
fallow garden, falling. Even the fly
with spotted wings needs sleep else it forgets
to fly toward what it most desires. I
wanted you to meet him, my guardian. I
wanted you to hear the sirens I heard. I
wanted you to see the electric pole suspended,
the bottom gone, the top half hanging after
the fire had passed, wires heavy, heavily
leaning toward the black ground, hot still. I've walked
on coals and not known because my long goose neck
bent, my beak at rest in my feathered back. My eye
open, not covered over like a brown bat
settling into his wings. Have you seen me sleep
like that? Maybe I'm an elephant. Maybe
I'm a giraffe. Maybe I need only half
the sleep my guardian needs. I see him fumble
behind his back and I choose the wrong hand.
He brings a finger out in front of him and points
at the wind I am to watch. He, cheat. I, dutifully.
It carries the canoe across the dead grass.
It lifts the roof off the chicken coop before

it dies down here, unhemispheric, here
hollow, like a goat, my guardian circles round
the mound of hay before he beds down, before he
shuts both his eyes. I take his still outstretched finger
and bring it to my mouth. I bite down.

7. (eighteen line poem for gordon)

He seems to me equal to gods that man
in my eyes, he seems like god's co-equal.
He'll hie me, par is he? The god divide me,
he seems able to dizzy me, to make my stomach empty.

If any museum had a postcard of Adonis,
in his absence, I went and collected it.
But even these could not rival the beauty
that sunders unhappy me from all my senses.

I mean to be always in his presence.
Him, who my limbs give into, whose limbs give into me.
We didst have chapped lips from kissing,
We didst miss classes because we fucked.
Both my eyes, like nights at noon, dark to all but him.

We didst marry. Leisure is dangerous
to me and it ruined fine cities but leisure
also in his eyes made orbs, made galaxies
and if I never let go his body grips me all
(greener than grass I am dead—or almost, I seem to me).

8.

We have a henhouse and a chick with a crooked
beak. She cannot eat, she cannot barely breathe.
We take her to the water, she resists, she shushes
to sleep. Ever naming is a blessing and a purse
nearly emptied. Our still-hatched hens don't lay.
I bring you to bear upon me, you see what I
could not before, affrighted, near thinking,
see. It's hard to stand on our own feet without
terror in our heels and aching in our hands,
Its hard, your body, bringing it to my mouth to speak.
Erection, is its best synonym, not relief.

9. (sleep restriction therapy)

At such heaviness I have something only
lighter than a pubic hair to give. Here.
I offer it to the sleep I no longer receive.
The body keeps making hollow promises.
It will echo back the silence it wants
but forgot how to hear, it will fall down dead,
eventually, it will bring me the sweetest melodies.
The difference between the intellect of a nest
and a bed must simply be the tree. Or the shade
it makes. Or the morning dove's call that in my
ear sounds like that of an owl. I am happy for it
the oblivion makes known another kind of poem,
the kind written in an attempt to fake the day
when the day can't be faked. One way of staying
awake: Make Catullus's lines into a sun of sorts,
make them perform. O Cock at his offal.
What you love that laves his teeth in pure water.
And it wants to purr in the public vulva?
Lethe is looking for me. Here, here I am!
I raise my hand, but it turns its course from me
and squats down in a run, wings tucked,
like a chicken that doesn't want to be caught.

10.

My hen hie went into her sawdust bed.
Before dawn, the sky blew itself straight through
puddles not gone, but a muddier roundness
to them that I might put my muck boots on.
That I might bring my God with me to bear
upon the ground pregnant with a child who
looks nothing like Him. That I might sing the days
of the week song. Wet hymn, the pen dirt webbed now
with four pronged claws. He's up on only three of them
and all the hens run. Damned universal cock,
as if the sun was blackamoor to bear your blazing tail.

11.

You wanna know how many of your fucks
would be over and enough for me, finally?
Our daughter has just learned of infinity.
She uses the word widely and loosely.
It's not a number, but a concept, I explain.
Indignant, she simply says, *oh yeah? show me!*
One Black Australorp laid 364
eggs in 365 days.
Fear not, you are worth more than the chickens.
Indeed the hairs on your head are all counted,
and multiplied. *That's* the number of times
That's what would satisfy your mad wife—

12.

Preternatural tree because look
at its leaves. Have you ever seen veins pulsing
like this? The wind may be the leaves' enemy
but day and night meet early, are meeting now
actually, both equally dignitaries
of this earth. The little brown bat who slept
for nineteen hours with half his thoughts on-
going is up. He likes the dusk. Who doesn't?
No cell is still at this hour so we traffic it,
the movement. We do not light a lamp, come
what may, its spring arms flayed, as if in embrace.

13.

I am trying to remember where I am
in time. Magna Mater giving birth on her throne.
Not supine and somehow between the known
and the unknown. That's where a baby, not yet breathing,
exists, on the verge of what we call being.
I look between my legs and see the bloody sheet.
Had we known now what we did then, our birthing
might have been upright and almost a relief.
Inexplicably, I think a thought I'll never need:
kills is the Dutch word for creek. That's not a thought,
I think. That's me seeing her breathe.

14.

One knows the dawn by the line drawn.
The burning ship on the horizon—the image
of terror and no way to get out there.
Tender holds both, not only an exchange
but a pain and the new love affair
beginning at birth but interrupted
by the amber alert. I search my body for my
children and they emerge. Today is full
of so many things tomorrow won't be. The sea
smoky, the Muderkill River contaminated,
and laundry. It comes to nothing. A relief.

15.

A branch sways in a breeze so slight it barely
moves the leaves. It rests heavy on the limb
of a neighboring tree. This is not a parable
about building one's house on sand or rock.
It is a fact that brings me to the base of the trees.
I find the sapwood exposed where they meet.
Before I can intervene, I think, *Intimacy!*
I say, *Hastily.* This is why I distrust myself.
Both branches creak. A sloth moves so slowly
his fur proves a welcome home for moths and algae.
He'd know better than me what's between the trees.

16.

The day I hold you in my arms, hens, one egg
feeds two babes: one likes the yolk, the other likes
the white, but one egg is not the same once
separated. I press you to my breast, chickens.
The day before that, I tripped on the raccoon
trap and cut my calf. What I fetched—the sex,
the body next to me in bed, the water
down the drain, the rattlesnakes, etc.—
immediately fled. Bereft, I brought all
my loves back and laid them on the grass. Like
hairs, each one gleaming there in the sun.

17.

Icy Jovian moon, I will not say veins
to you. The raccoon is in the trap now,
brown back blued by the light of our moon, full.
Tomorrow we will skin him, which we wouldn't do
but that every few days, the chicken head,
the feathered ground, *my hen,* she screams from the pen.
My hen nothing to be found. He will be bald
like you, Icy Jovian moon. But this mid-
night his pelt whelm him, loam I mean, silt still
chopped straw, humus, we dig our feet in,
by we I mean humans, raccoons, roosters, hens.

18.

Practice this sound: quietness. It looks like the flight
of birds or the lake in which they dip down.
Put your foot to the ground, one toe at a time.
Put your hand, not in or on, but with mine.
Try saying the word *tonsillectomy*. The word
being. This is the way I care for thee, empty
but in love. To pass the days in pain, the days
until you eat again, I research creatures
most endangered and we pray for them. We play
a game in which our efforts are combined.
Then was the fear a little quieted.

19. (sleep restriction therapy)

Uvulopalatopharyngoplasty
is an eleven syllable word for sleep
surgery. It is performed entirely
by opening my mommy body. I
repeat the word uvula eleven times:
uvula, uvula, uvula, uvu
la, uvula, uvula, uvula, u
vula, uvula, uvula, uvula
la. My speech accessory, my grape, my great
la la la vulva keeps me awake, keeps me
company, keeps my consonantal homewomb
happy, keeps me speaking from the throat. Tomorrow
we will burn the goat's horn buds to stubs. We
will need the morning light to do so. You
curled in bed, a u, a cradle at rest.
I put my head down on your pelvis, on your chest.
You breathe but do not speak. You don't even hear me
trilling. The vowel doesn't roll. A word. A stone.
An r. To be curved like you and unaware, I
put my mouth to yours and breathe your air.
The o shone. The o sang itself whole.
We ready the goat before the horizon lit gold.

20.

Everything seems to be saying that everywhere
something will be born today. The goat's moan
means nothing, apparently, though she keeps
looking back, trying to see around the bulge in her belly.
The yellows belong momentarily to the field,
to the hay, to her eyes that do not know what they
will soon see—the creature yellow too until she
cleans it, feeds it, finds his little hooves tender.
Everywhere says these things in unison,
almost silent in its insistence to bring forth
this little buck into its ever bearing world.

21.

Sweet honeybee, I'm sorry you died stinging me.
You left your intestines behind, but I'll cradle them
for awhile. This is radical autonomy
where the self isn't served, but the community.
Automatically, your lost barbed lance kills you
but me, cursing, momentarily reddened and itchy.
Sophocles said the dead, collectively,
sounds like a swarm of bees. My swollen finger
barely bends to make the poem. *Won't my mommy
be so proud of me?* Presumably,
the other bees are still making honey.

22.

The day before this day was all Sea of Galilee,
tumultuous and whatnot, but also freezing.
I rubbed their combs, feet, and beaks with vaseline.
The chickens', I mean. I nearly never hear the word
yesterday, which is when our target blew away.
The arrows don't know where to go. They just float.
When you haven't yet heard a word,
you're the brightest thing in sight. Even the waves obey.
I guess we can pass to the other side.
The storm is no longer furious,
and a certain portion of the pleasure is mine.

Hen Days

"The sun needs the moon, like the cock the hen."
—M. Maier, *Atlanta fugiens Oppenhiem,* 1618

I am at the sink again,
dawn and dusk, my hands sunk
in soapy water. I cannot bear to look
down at the dish I wash. The sheets
are in the laundry endlessly not because
we've dirtied them, but because the kids
have pinworms. What is an infestation,
the woodruff newly springeth,
the fowles singeth and perhaps my body too.
Its slippery. This day spent like all others
but for your tongue. Bring me a thousand kisses,
then a hundred, then a thousand more,
a second hundred. Bring me,
before they return, to the dirty ground.
The filth surround. I don't want anything
to ever be clean again, especially me.
Bring the threstelcock scoldeth oo
and bring me to the woods ringing.
Why must we wait until they look no more
out the doors at us. Now is their winter
woe gone, bring them away but quickly bring
the cock off flocking his hens
home while the water drains
and bring my shaking hands still
to the button of your pants.

All spring
we watch the magpies build their nest.
We watch the male try to impress his mate
by hefting large twigs above his head, then,

to the ground again, with care, repeatedly
for some unnumbered centuries. You
don't have to impress me. Just teach them
to say *please*. Please me. The rose rayleth her rode,
the leaves on the lythe wode. These birds
seem made of day and night equally, but without
a grey feather in between, without dusk or dawn.
The sky is heavy. It holds a place out to me.
The nest, like the toddler's palm
upturned, outstretched, is a hollowed curiosity full
of hungry mouths. Wormes woweth undercloud.
You: she and he both, cock and hen,
don't go, and if you do, come again speedily.

          Bees in wood,
in time, in solving terms, in trees deeper
into the pines shaken the spring storm taken
in one's hand, the leaves on the trembling trees,
penis, horny growth sheathed keep not thy silence,
god or dog or whatever it is that gets me off. Behave!
Leave my constant quarrelling with myself in bed.
I'm not one to be like trees shaken in the spring storm
with limbs fallen or taken in one's hand. Let nothing stand
still. Everything is flit. The daylily is lovely to see,
though her time is not mine.
The fenyl and the fille. The honeysuckle.
The clit daylit if we push the rotting hay away
and lie down on the wet ground, the new shoots
light green white coming up out to surround,
a littoral young and soft. Clitoral. The tongue sees
what would otherwise only be
felt. Eggs laid in the field, buried under
or burrowed over or borrowed without knowing
that all this bliss bryngeth dayes eyes in this dales, delight.

            Some higher hive
calls me. Some ritual excessiveness in which your body
is not enough and too much all at once. Imagine a circle,
its goodness not from beginning nor end. Describe (don't explain)
to the child: Joy in the middle of rejoice.
The plant, from fruit, derives its worth. The death, its life,
the word, its flesh. The jewel, its joy. Step
in: extend finger, wrist, ear, neck. The mone
mandeth hire lyht, So doth the semly sonne bryht.
The world so white with dew it looks like snow though
I'm warmed by it, adorned by it. The rabbit and I
are central to the garden. The rhubarb high
around his ear and my hip bones equally. He has more right
than me to be here, so he, still, watches us
as if not moving might be the protection
we all need. We spent yesterday in preparation.

            We
raked and mowed the leaves. We spread them evenly
over the garden. A great wind came and blew
them all away. Everything that grows or grazes knows
what territory truly means. My land, your body.
Egg, Pullet, Hen. Daylily, moon on the eaves.
Your eyes, like eggs, held up to the light:
A yolk in each eye! Let open
your body to me. Yoke, the day and the night both.

Acknowledgments

Thank you to the editors of the following journals for first publishing several of the Hendes poems: *Dusie, Kenyon Review, Northside Review, Interim, West Branch* and *Tupelo Quarterly.*

Thank you to Dancing Girl Press for publishing some of these poems in the chapbook *Thirty-Three Hendes.*

Thank you, Catullus. The Hendes series was inspired by Catullus's Hendecasyllabic poems. Though Catullus's form can't be easily translated because his meter depends on a series of long, short, and variable syllables, his poems are often translated into English in eleven-syllable lines.

Thank you to the authors (and translators) whose work I quote: Virgil, trans. H.R. Fairclough; the anonymous author of the Gospel of Matthew; Wallace Stevens; Eleni Sikelianos; David or Daniel or Nehemiah; Emerson Bennett; Catullus, trans. Peter Green and Louis Zukofsky; Martin Heidegger, trans. John Macquarrie and Edward Robinson; Henri Lefebvre, trans John Moore, and the anonymous author of "Lenten ys come with love to toune."

Thank you to my beloved friends and colleagues: Aby Kaupang, Matthew Cooperman, Camille Dungy, Julie Carr, Claudia Keelan, Becky Robinson, Kyle Schlesinger, and Dan and Kristy Beachy-Quick. Thank you to my dear friend, Haley Hasler, who painted the portrait of my family that appears on the cover of this book. Thank you to the animals and plants I tend. Thank you Rob, Gretchen and Erik Steensen, and thank you, most especially, Phoebe, Greta and Gordon Hadfield.

www.ingramcontent.com/pod-product-compliance
Lightning Source LLC
Chambersburg PA
CBHW022205080426
42734CB00006B/560